Original title:
In the Living Room of the Mind

Copyright © 2025 Creative Arts Management OÜ
All rights reserved.

Author: Cassandra Whitaker
ISBN HARDBACK: 978-1-80587-218-4
ISBN PAPERBACK: 978-1-80587-688-5

The Radiance of Unspoken Truths

In corners where thoughts like dust bunnies play,
They dance to the tune of old socks in dismay.
Each whisper and chuckle hides under a hat,
While the cat wears a frown at the end of the mat.

The couch holds its breath, it's a soft, squishy throne,
Where secrets are shared with a sigh and a groan.
The TV's a witness to tales that we spin,
As popcorn flies high from the bowl with a grin.

The lamp flickers gossip with every bright blare,
Casting shadows on laughter that hangs in the air.
We chuckle at wisdom that's wrapped up in fluff,
Finding joy in the moments that seem just enough.

So let us embrace all the quirks that we share,
In this bustling realm of thoughts laid out bare.
For the warmth and the wit are what make it a gem,
In this place where sanity bends, just like a hem.

Whispers Wrapped in Soft Light

The cat's plotting in shadows,
Nibbling on scattered thoughts.
The dog's confused by echoes,
Chasing tails of what's been wrought.

Laughter bouncing off the walls,
As socks begin to dance alone.
A chorus of whimsical calls,
In this cozy, chaotic zone.

The Harmony of Unfinished Sentences

Words hang like laundry on racks,
The punchline lost in a sock.
Ideas collide and then relax,
Like a sloth on a ticking clock.

Quirky jokes fly past the lamp,
Each thought a flickering light.
Scribbles swirl like a strange stamp,
Turning daydreams into night.

Navigating a Labyrinth of Ideas

Maps made of sticky notes cling,
To the walls of fleeting thought.
A mischievous muse takes wing,
In the puzzle my brain has wrought.

Lost in a maze of bright schemes,
Where the fridge hums a soft tune.
Reality bends with my dreams,
As I duel with the vacuum's swoon.

The Closet of Forgotten Dreams

Old plans tumble like folded clothes,
A musty scent of missed chances.
Daydreams peep out like shy toes,
Eager for thrilling romances.

Worn out wishes hang in the air,
Dust bunnies dance in each crack.
Whispers of futures we dare,
Hide beneath the forgotten stack.

Whispers of Quiet Corners

In the nook where socks do hide,
A dusty cat takes it in stride.
Chasing dreams of yarn and fluff,
A furry beast, it's just enough.

The shadows giggle, pots do clank,
Who knew a chair could be so dank?
Echoes of laughter fill the air,
As a couch potato claims their chair.

Shadows of Reflections

Mirrors hide the thoughts unsaid,
While the fridge hums a tune of bread.
In this space, ideas collide,
Like lost socks, they blush and hide.

Coffee cups dance on the floor,
As daydreams knock upon the door.
Pillows giggle, cushions sigh,
In this room, the mind runs high.

The Hearth of Thoughts

An armchair whispers tales of yore,
While crumbs of wisdom grace the floor.
Lamps flicker like intermittent jokes,
And curtains laugh at the cheeky folks.

In corners where the dust bunnies throng,
A radio plays an off-key song.
The tea kettle whistles, a mouthy friend,
As the tales of the heart never quite end.

Echoes of Solitude

A chair spins tales of solo fun,
While shadows chase the light of the sun.
Old books whisper secrets of past,
In this quiet, the moments last.

The playful clocks tick-rattle and hum,
With each tick, the giggles come.
In solitude, the mind takes flight,
Crafting stories in the waning light.

Fragments of Silence

In corners where thoughts trip,
A sock puppet debates the tip.
The fridge hums a funky tune,
While chairs gossip of the moon.

Dust bunnies dance, oh what a sight,
As spoons argue 'bout their flight.
The cat stalks shadows, king of his rule,
While I just laugh, feeling quite the fool.

Portraits of Inner Realities

Canvas of dreams splashed with hues,
Where wild ideas often muse.
A clock tick-tocks in rhythm divine,
While cookies contest with glass of wine.

Pillows engage in deep discourse,
As television shows plot their course.
The rug nods in approval, quite wise,
While I ponder, listening to the sighs.

The Coffee Table Chronicles

Upon this table tales unfold,
Of distant lands and heroes bold.
Cups filled, both empty and full,
Where laughter echoes, never dull.

Coasters whisper secrets of spills,
As the remote controls all the thrills.
Gathered memories clutter the space,
A treasure trove of light-hearted grace.

Comfort in Contemplation

Amidst the cushions thoughts collide,
Where mischief and nostalgia glide.
A book yawns, pages waiting,
While the mouse scurries, contemplating.

The lamp flickers, a friendly nod,
As shadows perform, oh what a prod!
Here in space where laughter blooms,
Life is lighter in these little rooms.

The Calm Within Turmoil

In a world where madness swirls,
I find my peace among the curls.
A sock insists it's a lost cat,
While my thoughts dance like a cheeky brat.

Chaos reigns on the coffee table,
A jigsaw puzzled yet still able.
The TV flickers with news so dire,
While I just want to build a fire.

Stacks of Unraveled Ideas

Papers pile like a mountain high,
A masterpiece—or a pumpkin pie.
Each thought a slice, a tasty treat,
But my muse has gone out for a tweet.

Sticky notes in a glorious mess,
Dreams jostling for some success.
One says 'dance,' the other, 'sneak,'
Leave it to me, I'll just take a peek.

The Cradle of Contemplation

In the corner sits a thinking chair,
It sighs and whispers all my care.
Should I nap or tackle to-do?
Turns out, I'd rather just watch blue goo.

Ideas drift like feathers in air,
One's a fish, another a bear.
They play tag, then climb a tree,
While I sip tea and let thoughts be.

A Canopy of Choices

Under bright thoughts that bloom like flowers,
I giggle at life's minute powers.
Should I bake or dive into a book?
Oh look—a squirrel giving me a look!

Decisions hang like laundry in breeze,
One whispers softly, 'You've got ease!'
But snacks call louder, oh what a fuss,
In this grand circus, I shall trust.

A Symphony of Stillness

Socks in the corner, they'll never unite,
A chair is a throne, where kings lose their might.
Dust bunnies waltz, with grace they do glide,
As echoes of laughter from curtains do hide.

Remotes have staged battles, they fight for the view,
With popcorn for armor, they're ready to chew.
Such chaos of silence, a war never seen,
The couch sighs in relief, it's a soft, cushy dream.

Secrets Beneath the Surface

The tablecloth whispers of crumbs and old stains,
While coats make a fortress, like long-forgotten chains.
A cat on the windowsill, plotting a caper,
Watches with glee as the dog makes a taper.

Beneath the old cushions, a treasure might hide,
Did someone lose something? Or is it just pride?
Old tea cups and memories, they linger about,
Each tale more ridiculous, the twist of a snout.

Imagined Gatherings

Imaginary friends sit around for a chat,
Debating the merits of cheese versus fat.
The lamp is a beacon, it holds all the fun,
While shadows are gossiping, plotting, and spun.

Chairs pulling close in a raucous delight,
Each voice chiming in, till there's laughter in flight.
Oh, do pass the pillows, we need softer sights,
For truths are best spoken on fluffy, soft nights.

The Rug of Reveries

The rug tells of journeys in patterns so bright,
With spots from the snacks that were dropped in the night.

It cushions the tumbling of thoughts in a race,
As doodles in corners find their rightful place.

A table of dreams, with imagination brewed,
With coasters as witnesses to stories accrued.
The ceiling holds secrets—where did they go?
As pillows conspire and the giggles will grow.

The Illumination of Insight

Bright ideas flop like fish on land,
Thoughts tumble out, never quite planned.
A lightbulb flickers, then dims real fast,
Like jokes at parties nobody asked.

Memory antics play hide and seek,
With wisdom that teeters, feeling quite weak.
A snicker here, a chuckle there,
Insights explode like popcorn in air.

Gleaming thoughts like a firefly's dance,
Catch them quick, give absurdity a chance.
Laughter ignites every corner's space,
In the clutter of ideas, we find our place.

Forgotten Boxes of Dreams

Dusty boxes piled up in a pile,
Dreams long lost, though they once had style.
What treasures lie in this mental junk?
A rogue unicorn, a dancing funk.

Socks that match with absent grace,
Rubber chickens in their right place.
Each box whispers a tale or two,
Of pursuits that went askew.

Wrapped in laughter with ribbons of cheer,
A thought pops up, 'Oh, I left that gear!'
Among the clutter, we find delight,
In forgotten dreams that bring us light.

The Warmth of Whispered Thoughts

Whispers twirl in a cozy nook,
Carried softly like an old storybook.
They giggle and dance, spreading like fire,
Turning half-baked musings into desire.

Hide-and-seek among pillows soft,
A tickle of nonsense, time gets aloft.
Ideas rustle like leaves on the ground,
In this chatter, absurdity found.

So let's sip tea, let thoughts unspool,
In this warmth, we break every rule.
Collect the whispers, stack them high,
Until laughter escapes—a jubilant sigh.

The Joy of Musing

Musings come with a twist and a shout,
Like gummy bears figuring out.
A riddle today? Who knows what's next?
Thoughts tumble like socks, totally vexed.

Here goes a rainbow, a cat with a hat,
Nibbling on dreams while wearing that.
In this carnival of mind so free,
No logical end, just pure jubilee.

With cackles and quirks in every thought,
We jive with ideas, wild yet caught.
In tangled webs of what could be,
We laugh at the sheer absurdity.

Between the Cushions of Time

Lost a sock, a time quite odd,
Between couch creases, who is God?
Thoughts tumble out, they make a mess,
While popcorn whispers, 'We digress.'

Chasing dreams that slip and slide,
On cushions soft, I take a ride.
There's a cat that's plotting schemes,
While I just nap and count my dreams.

Dialogues with the Self

Talking to me, he's quite a brat,
Argues loudly, 'Wear that hat!'
While I sip tea, he shares his plan,
To wear pink pants, and prance like a man.

I tell him, 'Dude, that's not the style!'
He winks and says, 'You lack my guile.'
With every sip, the banter flows,
Though deep inside, I wear his clothes.

The Window of Possibility

Peeking through this glass so clear,
I wonder if my cat can steer.
Beyond the frame, a dance, a whirl,
While squirrels plot their nutty burl.

I could leap to dreams untold,
Or stay inside, feeling bold.
The window creaks, the curtains sway,
I laugh and think, 'What a day!'

The Quietude of Understanding

Here we sit, in cozy chairs,
Mumbling thoughts, like hedgehog stares.
In silence, we share goofy grins,
As laughter erupts, everyone's wins.

We ponder life and cats so wise,
As they plot world domination, surprise!
In stillness found, with chuckles clear,
Understanding grows, spiked with cheer.

Frayed Edges of Memory

Forgotten socks in corners hide,
A wisdom lost, where dreams collide.
The cat's expressions tell a tale,
Of skewed perspectives, big and frail.

The clock ticks loud, it seems to mock,
How time just flies, like a wayward flock.
I laugh at ghosts of to-do lists,
Their scribbles fade in mists of twists.

The Palette of Emotions

Crayons spilled upon the floor,
A riot of hues behind the door.
I mix my colors, splash them wide,
In laughter's glow, my fears subside.

The deep blues dance, the yellows cheer,
A canvas bright, no room for fear.
With every stroke, a silly face,
My heart leaps up, a happy race.

Murmurs beneath the Surface

Whispers sneaking through the cracks,
Old jokes haunt among the snacks.
The cushions laugh, they know too well,
Of all the stories we can't tell.

A hidden giggle, a shrug, a sigh,
The fishbowl watches, yet it's shy.
Each thought a bubble, pops and flies,
Beneath the surface, laughter lies.

The Meeting Place of All Thoughts

A jigsaw puzzle missing pieces,
Thoughts wander off, like little creases.
Here's a sandwich, here's a shoe,
A tangled yarn that once was blue.

The mind is like a crowded street,
Where every car is fun and sweet.
We honk and wave, but often swerve,
In this chaotic, joyful serve.

A Tapestry of Tangled Ideas

Thoughts bounce like rubber balls,
Ideas wrapped in colorful shawls.
Jokes hidden in the couch's seam,
Whispering softly, a giggling dream.

Every cushion a secret place,
Hosting laughter's warm embrace.
A squirrel in a woolen hat,
Dances around like a silly cat.

Sticky notes in chaotic lines,
The cat debates the best of wines.
A toddler's scribble on the wall,
Creates a masterpiece, oh so tall.

Imaginary tea parties arise,
With no one there but our own sighs.
Laughter spills like spilled milk bright,
In this tangled world, nothing seems right.

Chasing Shadows on Gentle Walls

Shadows play with whispers neat,
Chasing echoes on sticky seat.
A sock puppet plots a grand scheme,
While paperclips dance and gleam.

A lamp collects tales untold,
Of strange whims and treasures bold.
Where do lost socks go at night?
A sock convention? What a sight!

Furniture hums with secret tunes,
As night descends beneath the moons.
Chasing shadows, we trip and laugh,
In a world of our quirky craft.

Old tapes try to argue with time,
Singing jingles, attempting to rhyme.
In our quirky, jumbled hall,
Funny echoes bounce off the wall.

Where Memories Sit in Silence

Dust bunnies gather, keeping score,
Of all the antics played before.
A chair snores softly, what a thrill,
It dreams of adventures, wait, do sit still!

The rug knows where the crumbs reside,
Each secret it has no one can hide.
Beneath the table, whispers flare,
Telling tales of who sat there.

Old photographs haunt the shelf,
Staring back at a younger self.
Tickling memories come to play,
Making us chuckle in a silly way.

A micro-mouse scampers by,
On a quest for crumbs, oh my, oh my.
In this sanctuary where we dwell,
Laughter echoes under the spell.

The Couch of Cognitive Currents

The couch hums a wild refrain,
Where thoughts and laughter intertwine, no pain.
Silly reminders gather like friends,
Each wrinkle hides where fun never ends.

TV remotes flow like streams,
Leading to unpredictable dreams.
Gummy bears plotting a heist,
In your pocket? There's still more rice!

The dog barks at philosophical air,
Lost in debates, I swear, I swear!
Tick-tock goes the wise old clock,
As thoughts run wild and never stop.

Pillows stuffed with jester's glee,
In a world as strange as can be.
In this flow of current delight,
We dance the weirdness of the night.

The Unseen Conversations

Socks are debating where to hide,
A turtle chimes in with wisdom applied.
Couch cushions whisper secrets and tales,
While the clock ticks softly, time never fails.

The cat plots escape from mundane routine,
While the dog looks on, blissfully unseen.
Dust bunnies argue, a furry debate,
In this quiet corner, they contemplate fate.

Thoughts take flight on wings of the absurd,
As the coffee pot brews with a giddy word.
Mugs chuckle loudly, a playful crew,
Imagined banter, always something new.

At last, it's decided, who reigns supreme,
In the gathering place of a fanciful dream.
With laughter and chaos, each day they greet,
A sitcom unfolds in this cozy seat.

Patterns in the Stillness

Patterns are dancing on the wallpaper,
While the blinds whisper secrets like a draper.
Cushions wiggle with a comical flair,
As the houseplants gossip without a care.

The rug giggles at every misstep,
While the lamp plays DJ with a soft pep.
Books debate genres like teams in a game,
Some cheer for tales, others seek fame.

The clock's hands tick-tock in comical haste,
While the fridge hums tunes with a cold taste.
In this gallery of wits and of quirks,
Every object converses, their fun works.

So sit back and jest in this funny space,
Where silliness dances with utmost grace.
Minds spin in circles, ideas take flight,
In the stillness, joy's hidden delight.

The Nest of Impulses

A hamster starts spinning his wheel of thought,
As the rabbit debates, pro and con, he's caught.
The fish bubble secrets in colorful hues,
While the air freshener sings, spreading good news.

Remote controls argue, who rules the screen,
As crumbs ponder paths that remain unseen.
Pillows embrace like old friends in a hug,
While the nightlight beams and gives them a snug.

Dreams bounce around like popcorn in bowls,
While the bookshelf wiggles with stories untold.
Each impulse nests like birds in a tree,
Creating a ruckus, inviting some glee.

In this whimsical haven, each thought unfolds,
Where laughter ignites and joy proudly holds.
Life is a circus, a play on the stage,
In the nest of impulses, we turn a new page.

Scribbles on the Canvas of Life

Art supplies chatter in a colorful spree,
Pencils and brushes at playful decree.
Canvas awaits with a blank, eager face,
While colors debate the best way to race.

Markers argue rainbow versus black gloom,
As glue sticks stick tightly in colorful room.
Paper crinkles with laughter, a giggling sound,
Where imagination scribbles freely around.

Mistakes are just humor in paint splatters bright,
Turns chaos to beauty, a joyous delight.
Each stroke is a story, each hue, a good laugh,
In the scribbles of life, we find our own path.

So let's grab our palette, our worries take flight,
Creating a masterpiece day and through night.
In the grand gallery where jest takes its stand,
Life's canvas unfolds, free and unplanned.

Framed Moments of Stillness

On the wall hangs a picture,
Of my cat in a hat.
He poses quite grandly,
With a look that's so fat.

My couch is a throne,
Of remote controls stacked.
Each button a journey,
To see what I've tracked.

The plants seem to gossip,
With leaves all a-flutter.
They whisper sweet secrets,
In the sunbeam's buttery.

The clock ticks in laughter,
As time does a jig.
I ponder the meaning,
Of pizza so big.

The Coffee Mug of Contemplation

In my mug sits a potion,
Dark liquid delight.
I ponder its essence,
As I take a big bite.

Steam rising like whispers,
Of dreams yet to brew.
Each sip holds a secret,
Or maybe just two.

The kitchen clock chuckles,
At my caffeine quest.
Froth swirls like my thoughts,
While I snack on a pest.

The cat sprawls beside me,
In a sunbeam's embrace.
I sip and I snicker,
At life's silly chase.

Sipping Serenity from a Quiet Cup

A teacup of calmness,
Whispers soft and slow.
Each sip tells a story,
In a warm, gentle flow.

Cream swirls like laughter,
As I muse on the day.
The milk is a dancer,
In a steamy ballet.

A biscuit's my partner,
In this quiet waltz.
Together we crinkle,
In the scones, no faults.

The world fades to shadow,
With each playful dip.
In this moment of stillness,
I find my sweet grip.

Threads of Emotion in the Fabric of Thought

My mind is a quilt,
Seamed with shades of glee.
Each patch tells a story,
Of the day, you see.

The bright prints of laughter,
With polka dots so bright.
Cuddle up in this comfort,
In the softest of light.

A thread of confusion,
Runs slightly askew.
I tug on the fabric,
To see what is true.

Yet humor is woven,
Through each tangled line.
In this cozy chaos,
I find joy that's divine.

The Chamber of Explorations

Within my thoughts, a door ajar,
I stumble in, my thoughts bizarre.
A penguin dances, a cat with flair,
They sip their tea without a care.

Each corner hides a silly scene,
A jester laughs, a frog in green.
A circus here, a bandit there,
My mind's a show, beyond compare.

A Retreat for the Imagination

Upon my couch, I take a seat,
A llama sings, it can't be beat.
A plant in shades of purple hues,
Recites the funniest of news.

With pillows stacked like mountain peaks,
The sofa speaks in different squeaks.
A chair remarks with wise old prattle,
While I just grin at this fine battle.

Moments That Linger

Each thought a bubble, floating high,
A squirrel in shades of pink walks by.
It spins a tale, it makes me laugh,
A giant cake—yes, that's its path.

With every whim and wacky ploy,
The hiccuping sounds of purest joy.
A fleeting glance, a wink, a nudge,
In this small space, we'll never budge.

The Flicker of a Candle

A flicker dances in the air,
A sock puppet fixed, a moody glare.
It tells a story, oh so bright,
Of socks that stole away the night.

With shadows stretching on the wall,
A worm in glasses starts to crawl.
It shouts, 'Excuse me, can I join?'
Raise a mug, it's time to coin!

Shades of Inner Chaos

Cushions piled high like mountains,
Remote controls in strange fountains.
The cat finds a comfy chair,
While I lose socks in thin air.

Thoughts bounce around in full spree,
TV static is my decree.
Puzzles of my crazy brain,
Dance like raindrops on a train.

Coffee spills and laughter breaks,
Finding snacks in oddest flakes.
Weaving tales of absent fame,
While goldfish swim in silence lame.

Oh, the echo of my delight,
As chaos reigns into the night.
With every laugh, a new mistake,
My mind's a jigsaw, wide awake.

Traces of Light in Shadows

Sunbeams filter through the blinds,
Tickling thoughts of silly kinds.
Ghosts of laughter haunt the space,
As I trip over a shoelace.

Mismatched socks on the floor gleam,
They dance like stars in a dream.
A plant with a curious grin,
Wonders where my brain has been.

Mirrors reflecting silly faces,
Pirouettes in awkward places.
Whispers of joy, a giggly choir,
Ignite the room with fun's own fire.

Thoughts glide softly, goofy and wide,
On this chaotic joyride.
In every corner, laughter calls,
As I gather life's strange, silly sprawls.

The Flicker of Ambience

A glow from the screen, a soft hum,
Creatures of comfort, they dance and strum.
While I search for the remote's hand,
A mission that's never quite planned.

Chairs lean back with playful creaks,
Disguising secrets the sofa leaks.
As snacks explode in a joyful spree,
The cat claims the best spot with glee.

Echoes of chatter fill the air,
As socks play hide-and-seek without care.
In this realm of silly delight,
Chaos wraps us up tight at night.

The flicker of thoughts starts to rise,
In this madness, we laugh and reprise.
With every grin, a new story spins,
In this bubble where humor begins.

Threads of Reflection

Old magazines lay scattered about,
With hairstyles that make me want to shout.
Reflections of a time long past,
Kick up a giggle, a joy that lasts.

Cups half-full of forgotten tea,
Hold memories of who we might be.
As stuffed animals ruminate,
About their dreams, it's never too late.

Fuzzy socks slip on the floor,
Faint whispers from the cupboard door.
Thoughts tied up with ribbon and flair,
All slip and slide without a care.

In this silly realm of mirth,
Every item counts, has its worth.
Through laughter, the chaos unwinds,
An enchanted space for our minds.

Shadows Dancing on the Walls of Yesterday

Shadows prance like lively sprites,
Chasing dust in fading lights.
Laughter echoes off the floors,
As memories slip through open doors.

Ghosts of jokes that time forgot,
Twist and turn in a wobbly plot.
They tickle thoughts with playful grace,
In this odd, enchanted place.

Cracks in the Imagination's Foundation

A creaky mind with plaster flaws,
Holds stories stuck without applause.
Each crack whispers a curious tale,
Of rubber chickens and a snail's wail.

Thoughts bounce off the left-hand wall,
As upside-down dreams begin to sprawl.
The universe giggles, a cosmic prank,
Inside this quirky, limping tank.

Colors of Feelings in a Hidden Palette

Feelings swirl like paint on a plate,
Mixing shades in a charming state.
Joy is lemon, sadness a gray,
While madness dances in bright array.

Silly blues with a splash of red,
Make perfect portraits of what's left unsaid.
Serious faces painted with glee,
In this masterpiece, we are free.

Navigating the Maze of Inner Stillness

A labyrinth of thoughts with twists and bends,
Where silence is louder than all your friends.
Each corner turned is a riddle, a jest,
Testing patience, putting minds to the test.

Lost in a tangle of fleeting bliss,
With thoughts that swirl like a pop song's tryst.
When laughter erupts from the depth of the drift,
You realize silence is indeed a gift.

Dusty Corners of Reflection

In the corners, shadows loom,
A sock lost to the vacuum's doom.
Thoughts gather dust, like old CDs,
Playing tunes that make us sneeze.

An armchair creaks, it tells a tale,
Of snack assaults and Netflix trails.
A cat curls up, as if to say,
"This mental mess is just my play!"

With papers tossed, like autumn leaves,
I ponder all my grand believes.
A coffee mug with witty quotes,
Sips from dreams like silly boats.

So here I sit, in messy glee,
Untangling thoughts like yarn from flea.
This chaotic view - is it profound?
Or just my mind's jumbled playground?

Echoes of Comfort and Chaos

In a corner, laughter echoes loud,
As the laundry piles, a fluffy cloud.
Memories dance like socks in air,
A silly ballet, beyond compare.

The TV blares with talk show frights,
While dishes stack to dizzy heights.
I sip my coffee, a blissful grin,
Waging war against the din.

Friends drop by, with tales to share,
We sift through chaos, without a care.
A blanket fort shields us from the stress,
Where laughter's armor finds its best.

So here we sit, on this lumpy floor,
With snacks that surely started a war.
In this wild world of comfort and fun,
We find our peace, though chaos has won.

The Canvas of Quiet Whispers

Brush strokes of chatter paint the air,
As muted giggles twist my hair.
Thoughts like polka dots, all aisles wide,
Whisper loud when no friends abide.

The three-legged chair squeaks out a tune,
As shadows waltz beneath the moon.
I narrate tales to an empty room,
Where pigeons plot my foiled zoom.

Memories hang like art on the wall,
Some are crumpled, some stand tall.
Each one grins, in happy frames,
While dust bunnies play their little games.

So let me paint with thoughts so bright,
Each echo a splash, my canvas of light.
In this quiet hush, where whispers bloom,
I find laughter within the room.

Shelves stacked with Dreams and Doubts

On wooden shelves, dreams gather dust,
Among old toys and forgotten trust.
A trophy gleams, though I can't recall,
When my glory days seemed ten feet tall.

Doubts like paperweights sit quite snug,
In a snazzy mug, where wisdom's drug.
Each sip reflects good times we seek,
Yet fear awaits, sly and bleak.

A plant in the corner seeks its worth,
Clutching sunlight, for what it's worth.
With every twist, I muse on fate,
As laughter finds that perfect date.

So here I stack my whims and woes,
In cozy corners where chaos flows.
As socks go missing, and dreams take flight,
I smile at this mess, a welcomed sight.

The Nook of Nostalgia

In corners where old memories dwell,
The cat tells tales, and the dog just yells.
Socks of decades past lie in a heap,
While everyone else is sound asleep.

The TV plays reruns of life's great hits,
The popcorn's stale, but nobody sits.
Grandma's knitting needles dance in the air,
Making sweaters for pets, with style and flair.

A vintage vase holds a dusty bloom,
It whispers secrets of laughter and gloom.
A chair that squeaks holds stories of old,
About love and mischief, bold and untold.

With laughter that echoes off wobbly walls,
The clocks, they tick funny; no one hears the calls.
We toast with lemonade and reminisce,
In this nook of antics, it's pure bliss!

Conversations in the Quiet

The walls, they listen to secrets we share,
While silence giggles, throwing past glares.
A couch full of cushions, all squished and tossed,
Sometimes it seems like it's totally lost.

The clock laughs at us, its hands moving slow,
While we debate whether to nap or to go.
The plants are judging us, all green and spry,
Wondering how we still don't know why.

We chat with the shadows, they crack funny jokes,
As we sip our tea, pretending like folks.
With a wink and a nod, we conspire to dream,
In whispers of laughter, like poems that gleam.

Together we plot our escape from the room,
But the laughter binds us, like a warm plush loom.
Lost in the chatter, our worries are few,
In this quiet chaos, we find our true hue.

Inhabiting Intentions

Intentions wander like cats on a spree,
Prowling for mischief, elusive as can be.
One aims for fitness but collapses in snacks,
While daydreams dance like a cat with no tracks.

The planner's filled with to-dos in a row,
Yet starting the laundry feels like a no-show.
The couch whispers soft, "Why not just lay?"
And intentions get sleepy, quietly sway.

The fridge hums a tune, inviting and bright,
As leftovers plot for their last little bite.
"Let's survive the weekend," we cheerfully scheme,
While reality giggles, an elaborate dream.

And through all the chaos, we manage a grin,
Intentions may wander, but joy seems to win.
In the fabric of moments, we find our delight,
With laughter like sunlight, making it bright!

The Depth of the Couch

The couch is a portal, a quantum delight,
Where snacks disappear and time takes a flight.
Remote controls vanish, like socks in the wash,
While cushions conspire for a plush, comfy posh.

Beneath all the layers, crumbs of the past,
Echoes of laughter that just seem to last.
The depth of the couch holds stories untold,
Of epic movie nights and chips bought in gold.

We dive in for comfort, the cushions embrace,
While popcorn confetti dances in space.
The dog makes a bed of all our old fears,
As we laugh at the chaos through giggles and tears.

In this well of comfort, we dream without shame,
The couch is a champion; it wins every game.
With laughter and fluff, we relish the ride,
In the depths of the couch, our joys coincide!

Parlor of the Soul

A cat in my lap, a remote on the side,
My thoughts run wild, like a joyous tide.
Cookies on the table, crumbs in my hair,
Each day is a circus, and life's quite a fair.

The TV chimes loudly, the news brings a frown,
While sitcoms spin stories, I just laugh and clown.
Neighbors peek in, as I dance like a fool,
This parlor's my kingdom, and joy is the rule.

Jokes from the sofa, shared laughter with friends,
We giggle and tumble, the fun never ends.
Old tales that go round, new tales that begin,
In this cozy chaos, there's never a win.

As shadows cast dances from the flickering light,
I ponder my quirks in the stillness of night.
With laughter as wallpaper, I sit snug and whole,
Welcome to the parlor, deep within my soul.

The Armchair's Embrace

Nestled in cushions, I sway and I tilt,
Spilling my secrets, like a fountain of guilt.
The armchair it chuckles, so plush and so wide,
Bass notes from my snacks, let the giggles abide.

My cushioned confidant, sturdy and round,
Whispers of nonsense, delightful and sound.
Tales weave through fibers, thick and quite grand,
Here in our bubble, we both understand.

The cat yells at shadows, as the clockworks tick,
Jokes about daytime, it's all quite a trick.
Beverages sprawl, far from classy, I'm sure,
Yet here in this chair, I'm content to endure.

So raise up a cheer for the armchair we trust,
In laughter's embrace, life turns to pure dust.
With each belly laugh, and a snort here and there,
We brighten the corners, with love in the air.

Tapestries of the Subconscious

Colors and patterns swirl round in my head,
Weaving through daydreams, like threads on a thread.
Monkeys on unicycles, they dance in delight,
A parade of the quirky, all hidden from sight.

Socks on the ceiling, where did they go?
Why is my toaster now flirting with snow?
Tentacles of nonsense, in grand shades of green,
Life's puzzle unfolds, oh what could it mean?

I scribble my thoughts, as they flutter and flit,
Each words' a new canvas, with giggles a hit.
As I toss out my worries, they fly like a kite,
In this tapestry, fun takes glorious flight.

So let's paint the universe, with whimsies galore,
Creating a picture, where laughter can soar.
With silly distractions and stories we bind,
We laugh in the net, of this curious mind.

Lanterns of Insight

Beneath the bright lanterns, my thoughts start to glow,
Illuminating wonders, both fast and quite slow.
A squirrel in a tux, with a top hat so neat,
Prances through visions and makes life complete.

Puzzles spun loosely, like yarn on the floor,
Each thread tells of misfits, who've opened a door.
The flicker of humor, ignites with a spark,
Shadows have faces, and dance in the dark.

I wander through stories, exploring with glee,
Mapping out tangents for what's yet to be.
Each laugh is a lantern, a beacon so bright,
Guiding through chaos, and bringing delight.

So figure a recipe for joy and for fun,
Mix quirks with a splash, let's laugh till we run.
In the glow of the lanterns, new insights will flow,
Lighting up laughter, like stars in a show.

Flickering Memories

Tickles of laughter bounce all around,
Chasing old shadows without making a sound.
The cat on the rug, with her sassy pose,
Snores like a bear, and nobody knows.

An old rocking chair creaks with delight,
As secrets spill out in the soft, warm light.
Grandma's cookies float in the air,
While dad tells a tale about a lost bear.

The clock ticks on, but time seems to play,
With sketches of childhood from back in the day.
Mom's mismatched socks become fuzzy attire,
While uncles dance silly by the fireplace fire.

So here's to laughter, our silly old friend,
In wacky moments that never quite end.
Each flickering thought, like a firefly's glow,
Brightens the memories we cherish and know.

The Sofa of Sentiments

In the plush embrace of cushions galore,
We sink into giggles, who could ask for more?
Popcorn explosions, oh what a mess,
As we plot our escape with stealth and finesse.

The remote control can't be found again,
Under a blanket, there's a sandwich that's zen.
Imaginary kingdoms where dragons snooze,
On this sofa of quirks, we can never lose.

Chair leg propped, we're the kings of our block,
Bouncing ideas like a funny old clock.
Every snort of laughter and gleeful delight,
Turns everyday living into sheer comic plight.

So here we lounge, with snacks at the ready,
The sofa can hold more than a little bit heavy.
With a shout and a squeeze, our hearts are ablaze,
In the realm of our dreams, we giggle and graze.

Untamed Thoughts Dance

Thoughts do a jig like they're lost on the stage,
Twirling with whimsy, like a giddy page.
Dancers in pajamas, all wearing a grin,
Unruly reflections bursting from within.

The ceiling fan spins like a wacky old tune,
While socks full of colors plot their own boon.
In this mind of ours, hilarity reigns,
As ideas collect like a storm in the plains.

Bouncing off walls, our musings collide,
Each giggle a boat on a whimsical ride.
Lingering doubts take a backseat to cheer,
As untamed thoughts dance without any fear.

So let's raise a glass to this fanciful spree,
Where absurdities thrive as we giggle with glee.
In the chaos of joy, there's always a chance,
For laughter and fun in the wildest of dance.

The Shelf of Dreams

On the shelf where adventures all sit tight,
Whispers of wanderlust fill us with delight.
Book spines tale of absurd worlds unknown,
Where socks can speak and each pebble has grown.

A teapot bears witness to tales we're told,
Of gardens with creatures adorned in bold gold.
Magic in teacups and stories we share,
Where everyone laughs, and nothing's a scare.

Montages of mishaps that never grow old,
In the shelf of our dreams, we're daring and bold.
With a wink and a nod, we play like a child,
To chase after giggles with hearts that run wild.

So dust off the shelves, let the laughter take flight,
In this fantastical place, everything's bright.
Join us in journeys through the wild seams,
In the happy chaos of our woven dreams.

Echoing Laughter of Dreams

Whispers of giggles fill the air,
Socks on the ceiling, who put them there?
Chasing the cat, oh what a sight,
He dodges and weaves, a furry delight.

Pillows are mountains, we climb so high,
Jumping and tumbling, we touch the sky.
Imaginary friends join in the fun,
We laugh till it hurts, oh what a run!

A cloud of snacks floats just out of reach,
Popcorn confetti spills as we preach.
Jokes take off, fly like balloons,
In our circus of dreams, we sing silly tunes.

Laughter echoing, a sweet serenade,
We paint with silliness, unafraid.
In this space where nonsense is free,
We dance like no one, just you and me.

A Soft Spot for Secrets

Whispers of mischief dance in the breeze,
Under the cushions, secrets freeze.
A treasure map scribbled on an old napkin,
Leads to a snack, there's no time for slackin'.

Tickles of giggles tucked between walls,
Who's there to hear when laughter calls?
A biscuit brigade on a bold little quest,
Sneaking past naps, and we're feeling blessed.

Hiding in boxes, our tales take flight,
Imaginary beasts come out at night.
With a flick of a finger, they vanish away,
Leaving us grinning 'til the break of day.

Secrets of laughter, tucked in our hearts,
Sharing our whims, that's where it starts.
In this cozy nook where mirth feels alive,
We venture together, and we always thrive.

Remnants of Daydreams

A big red sofa, a kingdom divine,
Cozy cushions piled, oh isn't it fine?
Under the sunbeams, our ideas sprout,
Flying on rainbows, we shout and we pout.

Paint-splattered fingers from making a mess,
Doodles on pages, can't help but confess.
Monsters and robots join in our games,
Building a fortress, no two are the same.

Sipping hot cocoa with splashes of glee,
Marshmallows swimming, come take a peek!
Each sip is a giggle, sweetened with cheer,
Tales come alive as we dream without fear.

Remnants of laughter linger in the air,
A blanket of joy, snug and rare.
In this whimsical world, time has no end,
We're silly adventurers, just you and me, friend.

The Curtain of Uncertainty

Peeking behind, what's hiding in view?
A sock puppet show, a wild debut!
Knitting together moments of play,
Crafting new stories to brighten the day.

What's that noise? Is it drums made of cheese?
Or maybe it's giggles, carried on breeze.
The curtain flutters, we stand on our toes,
Ready for antics, anything goes!

In shadows we spot the mischievous cat,
With a sly little grin, he's ready for that.
Unraveling giggles, like yarn in a ball,
With every tickle, we rise and we fall.

So here we remain, in this playful spree,
A world of confusion, pure jubilee.
The curtain may sway, but we play with might,
In this space of whimsy, all feels just right.

Sheltered Whispers

Socks on the ceiling, what a sight,
My cat thinks he's a bird, takes flight.
The couch gobbles chips, what a shame,
I'll blame the remote; it's all part of the game.

Neighbors argue over who's too loud,
While I just giggle, feeling proud.
A pizza box stacked high as the sky,
My thoughts wandering off, oh my, oh my!

Invisible visitors play hide and seek,
With rhymes in the air that feel quite unique.
I laugh at the walls, they chuckle back,
Irony sharpens on this quirky track.

A dance in my chair as shadows prance,
In this whimsical world, I take a chance.
Every silly thought jostles for space,
Within this bubble, I find my place.

Layers of Sentient Space

Cushions conspire, they're plotting a prank,
Mismatched socks argue on the flank.
Books whisper secrets like gossiping friends,
While I ponder how this madness ends.

The clock ticks louder, out of phase,
I swear it winks in its own quirky ways.
Dust bunnies giggle, holding their breath,
As I trip on the memories left in their depth.

Chairs tell stories of awkward chats,
Echoing laughter from old acrobat cats.
I chase my own thoughts like a playful leaf,
In this playful realm, I find my relief.

A jigsaw of feelings, spontaneous fun,
Where every dilemma's a joke to be spun.
Here, silliness reigns, wrapped in warm hugs,
In the layers we live, no tight-fitting rugs.

The Rhythm of Unrest

My shoelaces dance like they've got a say,
In this raucous rhythm, they lead me astray.
Coffee cups waltz on the kitchen shelf,
Each sip a swirl, each thought a help.

Wires tangle into a modern art piece,
With frantic motions, no sign of peace.
The fridge hums softly, beats from the past,
It's a symphony growing, meant to last.

Cushions bounce with giggles so bright,
Their whispers tickle, oh what a sight!
My mind's a dance floor, full of surprise,
Where ideas do cartwheels and laughter flies.

The rhythm of chaos, a delightful show,
Where even the dust can put on a glow.
Life's strange ballet, so awkwardly sweet,
In the jumbled corners, we find our beat.

Meditations on the Mantel

Dust gathers wisdom like an old sage,
As I ponder life's quirks, flipping the page.
Pictures judge me from their ornate frames,
With smirks and frowns, they're calling me names.

Candles flicker like they know my thoughts,
Winking at troubles that life often brought.
A stack of magazines, piled up high,
Whispered opinions, oh my, oh my!

The clock strikes laughter, tick-tock like a joke,
As I sit cross-legged, just feeling the smoke.
Meditation is chaos wrapped in a bow,
A dance on the mantle where silly thoughts flow.

In this odd gallery, my mind takes a stroll,
Sipping on whimsy; it's how I roll.
The mantel holds treasures, both sweet and absurd,
In the giggles of silence, my laughter is heard.

Ashes of Yesterday's Conversations

In the corner, the cat naps,
Dreaming of fish and fancy traps.
While we debate, with fervent claims,
What really goes on in bed frames.

Cushions hold secrets and lies,
As laughter dances and softly flies.
Who said that joke, oh was it me?
Or just the ghost of my memory?

We spill our thoughts like tea on the floor,
Leaving stains that we can't ignore.
Each story told, another layer,
And who is the real instigator?

But as dust settles on our chat,
We smile and laugh, the joke is flat.
The ashes of laughter, they still remain,
In the echoes of our joyous refrain.

Reflections on the Coffee Table

On the table lies a coffee stain,
Remnant of laughter, a silly bane.
Reflected tales in porcelain cups,
Of clumsy trips and silly hiccups.

We gather 'round for a light jest,
Pretending we're surely the best at the quest.
Who made that pile of old magazines?
Is it treasure, or just what it seems?

Beneath these surfaces, lies a tale,
Of friendship, laughter, and a bit of fail.
Each creased page holds the weight of our fun,
In moments shared, under the sun.

A game of charades turns into a spree,
As we guess the wiggles of silly esprit.
Our coffee may cool, but hearts stay warm,
In reflections that dance, away from the norm.

Murmurs of Unsaid Words

Whispers float like dust in the air,
As thoughts bubble up, it's only fair.
Do we dare say what we both know?
Or let the silence take on a flow?

Unsaid words bounce like a ball,
Echoing softly through the hall.
Is it fear, or just lack of a cue?
As we ponder long, the evening's dew.

A quirked eyebrow tells so much more,
A chuckle stifled, behind closed door.
What should be spoken becomes a game,
With phrases hidden, it's all the same.

But laughter creeps through the unsaid space,
As we poke fun, in our goofy race.
Murmurs steady, turning into cheer,
In an unspoken bond that feels so dear.

The Rug Beneath Our Recollections

Beneath our feet, the rug lays thick,
Storing memories, both sweet and sick.
With every step, stories arise,
Unfolding laughter in playful guise.

It holds our secrets from long ago,
Each thread a network, a woven show.
A dance of feet and memories tight,
Shuffling through echoes, a silly sight.

Spilled popcorn kernels from movie night,
Or tripping over when things get tight.
The rug waves hello, a nostalgic greet,
With bumps and shags, it feels so sweet.

And as we gather, the memories weave,
With each laugh shared, it's hard to believe.
That underneath our playful play,
Lies the joy of yesterday's display.

The Embrace of Solace

Cushions fly as laughter bursts,
A cat on my lap, but she's not the worst.
Coffee spills from a mug with pride,
Oh, the chaos that lives inside!

A sock puppet show for one and all,
Dancing shoes? Nah, they just fall.
The TV's on with echoes of cheer,
It's a sitcom, or is it my beer?

Old memories bloom in a faded frame,
With every glance, nothing feels the same.
I chat with the ghosts of snacks long gone,
While pretending to work on my dawn.

Yet here among the clutter and cheer,
Each laugh and sigh brings my thoughts near.
In this mishmash of joy and jest,
I find a place that feels like rest.

The Artistry of Puzzle Pieces

Jigsaw bits scatter across the floor,
A spare tire? Or did I find more?
No image matches; round pegs in square,
As I grin at the chaos, not much to spare.

Unraveled threads of a sweater lost,
My tangled thoughts, at a hefty cost.
Yet here I am, engrossed in the fuss,
Creating art from a giant plus.

Tables turned, the clock strikes noon,
Puzzles dance to a whimsical tune.
With coffee cups and mismatched mates,
Who knew that solving could come with great fates?

I smile at the pieces that never fit,
Each oddball shape, a perfect bit.
In laughter's name, I carry on,
Who needs a roof when there's a song?

Tides of Self-Discovery

Waves of thoughts crash on the shore,
As I paddle through life, wanting more.
Surfboards made from dreams and doubt,
I ride the ups while trying to shout.

A beach ball bounces, off the wall,
Giggling hard, I may trip and fall.
Revealing truths in a tide pool's gleam,
Seeing my face in a frothy dream.

Shells of wisdom scatter near,
Each one shines as the end draws here.
In every crinkle, a new surprise,
Perhaps I'm wiser with cheery eyes.

And when the sun begins to dip,
I grab my thoughts like a messenger's ship.
On these tides, I glimpse the fun,
In self-discovery, we've just begun.

Thoughts Unraveled by the Firelight

In the corner, the flames flair high,
A marshmallow roast as friends drop by.
Stories unravel, they're zesty and bright,
We laugh till we're dizzy, it feels so right.

The shadows dance in their playful roles,
Each nod and wink warms our souls.
With silly secrets and tales so bold,
The night's like a tapestry, bright and gold.

Time slips away like ash in the breeze,
Who needs a clock when we're feeling at ease?
We craft up laughs, like a fine wine,
Here, in this moment, everything's divine.

As embers whisper their soft goodbyes,
We cherish each chuckle and each reprise.
In the warmth of this glow, we find our glee,
Unraveling thoughts that set us free.

Flickering Flames of Memory

In the corner, a cat takes a nap,
Dreaming of fish in a faraway map.
While the toast pops up, it's a real surprise,
As buttered toast flies straight for your eyes!

Grandma's stories echo, a comedic fright,
Like a dance with the shadows, in the flickering light.
She loses her glasses, again, what a game,
'They must be right here!' but it's really quite lame.

Friends gather 'round with a laugh and a cheer,
Swapping wild tales of their most awkward years.
Every memory's precious, but oh what a fright,
Especially those shared under the dimmed moonlight!

In this chaotic scene, joy is reborn,
As laughter fills spaces that once seemed torn.
Here's to the moments that make living sweet,
With flickering flames and a room full of heat!

Portraits of Perception

Each face in the room tells a story untold,
Like Jackson Pollock with antics so bold.
A sneeze here, a chuckle, a crash of old tea,
Spontaneous bursts of absurdity, whee!

The clock ticks away, but time takes a break,
When uncle starts rapping to a dog's silly shake.
A coffee cup sloshes, an artist's own fight,
With stains on the canvas, it's a masterpiece, right?

Father channels Picasso with wild flair,
A portrait of mother, with hair in the air.
The palette is chaos, but laughter ensures,
That beauty's perception can break all the boors!

So let's marvel at moments, from odd to the sweet,
In portraits of perception, life's messy but neat.
Art is alive and it's always unplanned,
Held together by laughter, and a warm, loving hand!

The Window to Unseen Realities

A window that shows what we wish to forget,
Like the neighbor's dog who had too much to bet.
Barking at shadows, it wags its great tail,
As the mailman sprints by with a squeal and a wail!

Peering through curtains, we see all the fun,
A wild symphony playing under the sun.
Perspectives collide, with incredible glee,
When a tumbleweed rolls into our tea!

Imagining worlds where the squirrels hold court,
With acorns as currency, they're quite the retort.
Every glance outside adds to our thrill,
And brilliant ideas come with each nip of chill.

So let's swing open windows with laughter and cheer,
For unseen adventures are waiting quite near.
Through panes of perception, we see humor's embrace,
In the wildness of life, there's plenty of space!

Swaying Curtains of Contemplation

Curtains that sway with a whimsical breeze,
Whispering secrets as they dance with ease.
Thoughts float around like a kite on a string,
As laughter erupts from the joy that they bring!

The sofa has stories that quilt us in dreams,
Of frogs in tuxedos and wild ice cream themes.
An old vinyl record plays scratchy delight,
With tunes that make even the chairs feel polite.

Pondering life while the teapot sings,
Imagining fish with a thousand small wings.
Watching the world through a whimsical lens,
Where silly and serious play as best friends!

So let laughter prevail in this quirky cocoon,
Where swaying curtains sway like a bright afternoon.
In contemplation's dance, we're free to explore,
The beauty of living, forever encore!

Softly Spoken Realities

Whispers dance in corners bright,
One sock sings a tune of fright.
The cat debates with the old lamp,
As shadows plot their cunning camp.

Cushions giggle, they know it all,
Dreams unfold, then gently fall.
The rug hides secrets, soft and sweet,
While the coffee pot sets the beat.

Chasing Thoughts Across the Room

I chase my thoughts like wayward flies,
They buzz and dart, oh what a surprise!
The clock laughs loud as time just teases,
While puppies roll, creating breezes.

An echo of a joke long past,
Leaves a grin that's unsurpassed.
Chairs conspire with playful creaks,
As my brain trips on silly peaks.

The Gallery of the Imagination

Art hangs crooked, a quirky scene,
Painted with dreams of what might have been.
The sofa sports a polka-dot,
It's hard to tell if it loves the spot.

Frames may shift with twisted glee,
While visitors sip some herbal tea.
Silliness amplifies every hue,
In this gallery, joy feels like a brew.

Coziness of Conflict

The dog debates with the chair-leg,
Stalemate's a wager, bet on a peg.
The blanket tags the footstool a thief,
While the remote stirs up disbelief.

Cushions strategize a soft revolt,
Muffled laughter is the result.
As the clock ticks on, they all conspire,
Creating a warmth that never tires.

www.ingramcontent.com/pod-product-compliance
Lightning Source LLC
Chambersburg PA
CBHW060114230426
43661CB00003B/177